INVESTIGATING
Body Systems

Investigating the
IMMUNE
SYSTEM

Natalie Hyde

A CRABTREE FOREST BOOK

Crabtree Publishing
crabtreebooks.com

Author: Natalie Hyde

Series research and development:
Natalie Hyde

Editorial director: Kathy Middleton

Editor: Ellen Rodger

Proofreader: Melissa Boyce

Design: Tammy McGarr

Print and production coordinator:
Katherine Berti

IMAGE CREDITS

Alamy: Science History Images p 27

iStock: Prostock-Studio p 7 (top); duncan1890
p 9 (top); AndreasReh p 10 (bottom); urfinguss p
11; JuSun p 12; YinYang p 29 (second from top);
sturti p 31 (top left); JodiJacobson p 31 (middle);
ParkerDeen p 35 (bottom); Drazen Zigic p 45
(bottom);

Shutterstock: CREATISTA p 31 (right);
Niloo p 36 (left); Sumit Saraswat p 39 (bottom);
xian-photos p 40; Akimov Igor p 42 (top)

Wikimedia Commons: Gallica Digital Library p 10
(top); Sir Charles Bell p 21 (bottom); Ernest Board
(1877-1934) p 24 (bottom)

Crabtree Publishing

crabtreebooks.com   800-387-7650
Copyright © 2023 Crabtree Publishing

Hardcover   978-1-0398-0648-1
Paperback   978-1-0398-0674-0
Ebook (pdf)   978-1-0398-0700-6
Epub   978-1-0398-0727-3

Published in Canada
Crabtree Publishing
616 Welland Avenue
St. Catharines, Ontario
L2M 5V6

Published in the United States
Crabtree Publishing
347 Fifth Avenue
Suite 1402-145
New York, NY 10016

Library and Archives Canada
Cataloguing in Publication
Available at the Library and Archives Canada

Library of Congress
Cataloging-in-Publication Data
Available at the Library of Congress

Printed in the U.S.A./012023/CG20220815

Contents

The Body's Security Alert

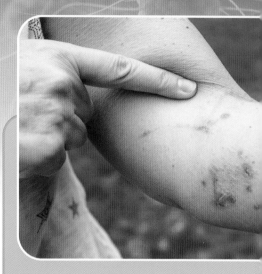

Summer is a great time to enjoy a weekend camping trip. Imagine setting up your tent and campfire in the woods. Suddenly, however, you start to see a red, itchy rash on your arms. Poison ivy! But why did that rash appear? And what is its purpose? The swelling, itching, and redness are all signs that one of the most important systems in your body is working—the immune system. Its job is to protect you from harmful invaders to your body.

All plants and animals have some form of immune system. The ability to survive against the attack of harmful **organisms** or elements is something all living things need. Without an immune system, the human body would be easily damaged by infection and disease. Our life spans would be short. Humans might not even exist as a **species**.

There are many individual viruses and **bacteria** around us every day. You cannot avoid coming into contact with them. There are about 100 million of them for every star in the universe. They are in the air, in water, and in the soil. Luckily, most of them are not a threat to humans, but the ones that are pose a great risk to our health.

What Does Contagious Mean?

A disease that can be passed on from one person to another is called contagious. Contagious diseases are spread when the **germs** from an infected person are transferred. This can be on surfaces that someone else touches, in the air where an infected person has coughed or sneezed, or in body fluids. That is why people have been advised to wear masks and wash their hands more often during the COVID-19 **pandemic**.

A rash is the body's reaction to the oily resin on poison ivy leaves that a person may brush against while hiking.

Cell Network

The immune system is not just found in one part of the body. It is a large network of cells, tissue, and organs that work together. You can think of it like a fort with guards. Organs such as the skin, as well as tissue and **mucus**, work like the stone walls and moat. They keep risky viruses and bacteria from entering the body. If invaders make it into the body, an alarm system activates the cells that kill and destroy the invaders.

Not all organisms that make it into the body are dangerous. In order to work well, the immune system has to be able to tell the difference between **beneficial** bacteria, such as the probiotics often found in yogurt, and threats such as Group A Streptococcus— which we know as strep throat. Guards on duty at a fort would shout "Friend or foe?" when someone new came to their gates.

Cells traveling through the bloodstream do the same thing. They inspect any outsiders and decide whether to arrest and detain them or let them go free.

It is not just infections and disease that are tackled by the immune system. It also deals with things such as allergies and intolerances. Intolerances are substances that our body might struggle to break down and absorb. Some people are intolerant to milk proteins, for example.

So how do you know that your immune system is at work? If you experience things such as chills, a runny nose, or a cough, you can be sure that your immune system is on duty. Fever and swelling are often the first signs the system has been **activated**.

The stone walls of a fort help keep invaders out. The body's walls are its skin and tissue.

Key Figures

Brigitte Alice Askonas is known as the "Grand Dame of Immunology." This is a term used to note a woman of great ability and respect. Askonas was a biochemist who worked at the National Institute for Medical Research in London, U.K. She became head of the immunology department, studying specialized immune cells called B cells to determine their role in the immune system. Askonas won several scientific prizes for her work.

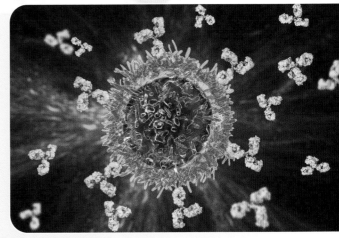

B cells are a type of white blood cell that makes **antibodies**. They are part of the immune system.

CHAPTER 1

How Do We Know?

Originally people believed that sickness was a punishment for being bad or not following religious laws. Sickness was often treated by healers or shamans who used spells and charms to get rid of bad spirits.

In Greece around 480 B.C.E., a Greek physician named Hippocrates began to question this idea. He thought that diseases had a natural or physical cause. He believed there were four fluids in the body, called humors, that needed to be kept in balance. Too much or too little of any of the fluids would make a person ill. Hippocrates thought doctors should be neat, calm, and honest with their patients. He even insisted they trim their fingernails and wash their hands. This was a new idea, as no one had thought about cleanliness having an effect on disease. Without knowing it, Hippocrates had come across one of the most important rules of preventing illness.

The worst diseases gave researchers insight into the body's own defense systems. During a **plague** in Greece in the 400s B.C.E., historian Thucydides wrote about people who recovered and were "immune" from getting it again. This was the first time the work of the immune system was recognized.

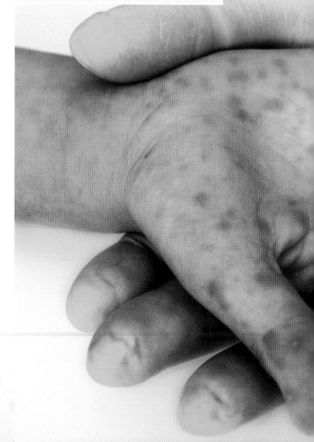

Hand, foot, and mouth disease is an infection caused by a virus. It leads to fevers and sores on hands, feet, and in the mouth.

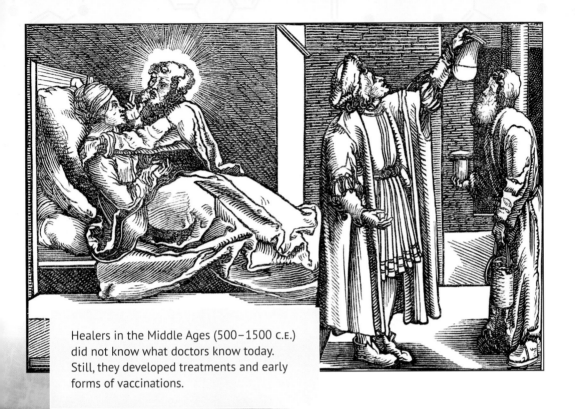

Healers in the Middle Ages (500–1500 C.E.) did not know what doctors know today. Still, they developed treatments and early forms of vaccinations.

Smallpox was a disease that could be traced as far back as ancient Egypt. It was the next disease to point to the existence of the immune system. Smallpox spread through China in the 900s C.E. as a result of trade and exploration. As it spread, people noticed that there were two variants, or forms, of the disease. One was more deadly than the other. The Chinese were the first people known to have tried "variolation." This was a process where scabs from someone suffering from the milder version were rubbed either on open sores or in the noses of healthy people. Variolation would give the healthy person a milder version of the disease and help them avoid death from the more severe version.

New Ways to Fight Disease

Smallpox was still causing deaths in 1796 when English doctor Edward Jenner noticed something curious. Milkmaids who were in contact with dairy cows were getting a similar but milder disease called cowpox. But they didn't seem to ever get smallpox. He suspected that cowpox could be used to protect against smallpox. In 1801, he published a paper called "On the Origin of the Vaccine Inoculation." In it he recommended **inoculation** with the cowpox virus to protect against the deadlier smallpox.

Vaccination by injecting a virus directly into the bloodstream replaced variolation. Scientists knew that it worked, but still didn't understand exactly how it worked. Discovering germs, or microscopic organisms, was the next important step in understanding immunity. Experiments done by French chemist Louis Pasteur confirmed that germs existed and that they could be killed by heat.

Jewish Ukrainian-Romanian scientist Élie Metchnikoff made the next major step in understanding the immune system. He identified the body's cells that surrounded and destroyed dangerous viruses or bacteria. These special cells, called phagocytes, could fight off dangerous viruses and bacteria called pathogens. This was the beginning of our understanding of **innate** immunity. This is the immunity that we are born with.

Next came the discovery by Emil von Behring showing that the body produced a Y-shaped protein called an antibody. Antibodies are produced by the body to kill one specific foreign substance. This could be a poisonous substance such as snake venom, or a certain pathogen such as the measles virus. Behring's studies showed that the body didn't only have cells you were born with to fight illness, but it also produced its own specialized ones. This is known as created or **acquired** immunity.

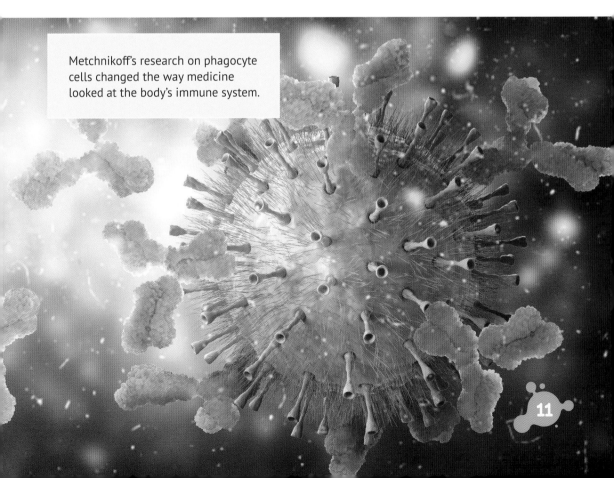

Metchnikoff's research on phagocyte cells changed the way medicine looked at the body's immune system.

Cells and Antibodies

Until the mid-1900s scientists had pieces of the puzzle of the immune system, but not the whole picture. New experiments showed that there wasn't just one type of antibody, there were many. The antibodies were very specific to the type of invader that they met. There also seemed to be cells in control that responded to threats and created the antibodies that were needed. The way these two types of cells worked together was called "clonal selection **theory**." This theory, first introduced in 1957, was a breakthrough in understanding how the immune system works.

In the mid-1900s, the connection between the lymphatic system and the immune system was discovered. The lymphatic system is a network of **nodes** and vessels found throughout the body. Lymph nodes are the size and shape of a kidney bean. The vessels are tiny tubes that move fluids. This is how many of the white blood cells are able to move around the body.

Key Figures

Sir Frank Macfarlane Burnet was an Australian doctor who specialized in virology, or the study of viruses. He published a paper in 1957 about his new theory: clonal selection. He felt this was "the most important thing I would ever do in science." Burnet won a Nobel Prize for Physiology or Medicine in 1960 for his work on immune response.

White blood cells move throughout the body via the lymphatic system.

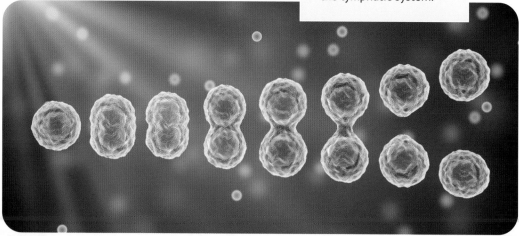

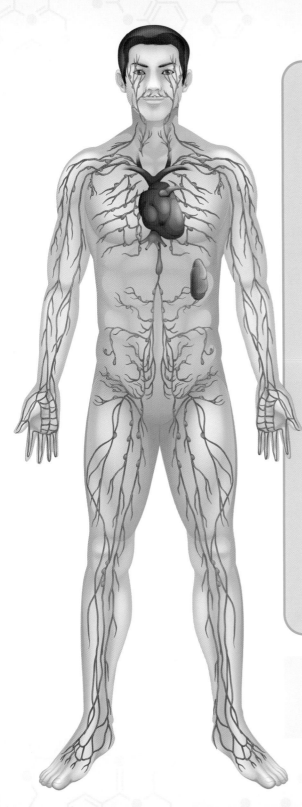

Clonal Selection Theory

Each type of germ has a different structure on its surface that helps it invade cells. This is called the receptor. Each different antibody in our system matches the shape of a certain receptor. When a dangerous virus or bacteria enters the body, special white blood cells identify it. These cells then signal for the specific antibodies that match the invader to start cloning, or copying. The immune system can produce millions of antibodies. These antibodies attach themselves to the receptors, which marks them for destruction. Other white blood cells move in and **eliminate** the marked invaders.

The lymphatic system is a network of vessels, tissue, and organs that is part of the body's circulatory system.

CHAPTER 2

The Immune System

The immune system contains two main parts: the innate or natural system, and the acquired system. We are all born with an innate immune system. Our innate immune system is inherited from our parents. It is active the moment we are born. Before birth, we are protected by our mother's immune system.

Our innate system starts with physical barriers to keep pathogens out. Pathogens are organisms that can cause disease, and include viruses, bacteria, fungi, and parasites such as worms. Our physical barriers include our skin, mucus in our nose, earwax, the coating on our eyes called the cornea, the lining of our stomach, our lungs, and our intestines. Tears and **saliva** can flush out pathogens that make it into our eyes or mouth. These all prevent pathogens from entering our bloodstream and making their way easily around our body where they can multiply and cause damage and illness.

White blood cells are the soldiers of the immune system. There are several different kinds. The innate immune system consists of a type of white blood cell called phagocytes. They patrol the blood, looking for invaders. When they recognize one, they send out a chemical signal calling other phagocytes to come to their location. Then they surround the invader and kill it. Thirty-three ounces (1 L) of human blood can contain about 6 billion phagocytes. These cells respond the same way to any invader they sense. They do not have cell memory so they do not provide long-lasting immunity to any one invader.

Some parasites cause diseases. The nematode parasite is passed to humans through the bite of a mosquito. It causes filariasis, which can lead to blindness.

Passive Immunity for Newborns

Passive immunity happens any time a person receives someone else's antibodies. Passive immunity is vital for newborn babies. Antibodies are passed between mother and child. This gives babies some protection until their own immune system begins functioning. Passive immunity usually only lasts a few weeks or months.

Newborns are protected by their mother's antibodies when they are born. A child's immune system is usually fully developed by age seven or eight.

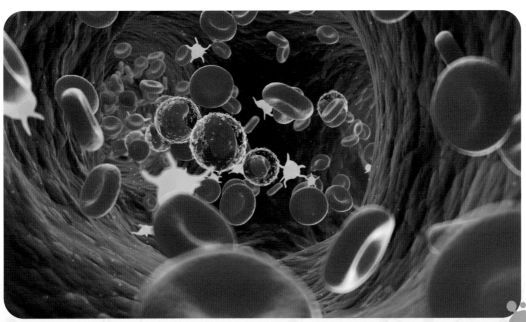

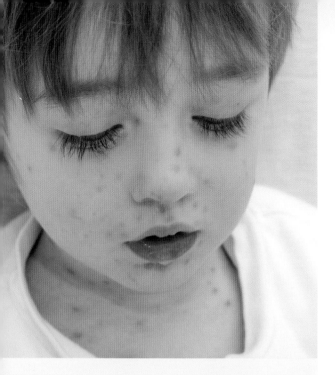

Chicken pox is caused by the varicella-zoster virus. Small, itchy blisters can cover all areas of a person's body. After infection, the virus remains in the body's nerve cells. The immune system usually keeps it under control. Later in life it can lead to a painful infection called shingles.

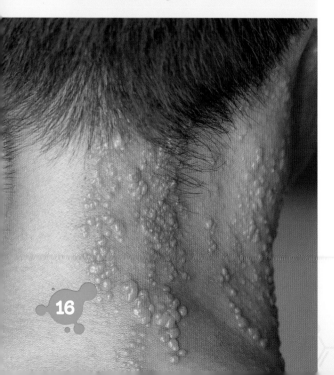

The Acquired Immune System

The innate immune system has limitations. It has no cell memory. That means it has to go through the process of recognizing a pathogen and signaling for help each time the invader attacks. This may leave the body at risk from a delay which allows the pathogen to multiply and spread. To help with this, our bodies have an acquired immune system.

Our acquired immune system is not up and running at birth. It is always changing because it develops over a lifetime. It is more specialized to deal with the millions of different types of pathogens that we meet every day.

The strength of the acquired immune system is its memory. The acquired immune system makes special proteins called antibodies. Each antibody has the job of attaching to one type of pathogen. This antibody is created only after your body has **encountered** the virus, bacteria, or other dangerous substance. For example, once you have been exposed to the chicken pox virus, your body will have antibodies against it. These antibodies are created in special white blood cells called B cells. B cells have helpers called T cells. T cells signal the body to rapidly make more antibodies. Even after the invader is eliminated antibodies stay in the body, and they can remember the pathogen. Because of this, the invader will be recognized as a threat more quickly.

Immunoglobulin Treatments

In some situations, people cannot produce their own immune response in time. Those at risk can be treated with antibodies obtained from animals or other people. They can also be produced in a laboratory for a specific disease or infection. For example, people bitten by venomous snakes are given antivenom, which is a mixture of antibodies against the type of snake venom they were exposed to.

Antivenom is traditionally made by collecting venom from snakes, spiders, or other animals that bite and inject venom. It must be used quickly after a bite to disable the venom.

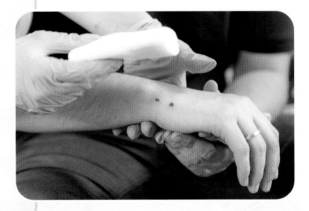

Better Together

The innate and acquired immune systems work together. Most of the time we don't even feel the immune system at work. It neutralizes, or makes invaders harmless, before they become a problem. It is constantly busy. Scientists know this because the immune system generates from 0.07 to 0.11 ounces (2 to 3 grams) of antibodies every day!

Cells of both parts of the immune system are made in many different parts of the body. Phagocytes, like most white blood cells, originate in bone marrow. Bone marrow is the soft, spongy tissue in the center of bones. B cells also develop there. T cells begin their development in the bone marrow, but then mature in the thymus. The thymus is a **gland** that sits between the lungs.

Once they have been created, cells of the immune system move to other locations to begin their work. Some white blood cells hang out in the lymph nodes, waiting for instruction to **replicate** and attack. To move around, they flow through the lymph vessels that are found throughout the body.

When a pathogen enters the body, the phagocytes of the innate system begin the body's defense by **engulfing** the invaders. The phagocytes then display pieces of protein of the invader on their surface. They send a chemical signal to the acquired immune system to come help. When the B and T cells arrive, they see the protein of the attacker and call up the antibody that matches that pathogen. If no memory of the invader exists, a new antibody has to be created and then replicated to kill off all invading cells.

IMMUNE RESPONSE

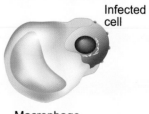

Infected cell

Macrophage

ORGANS OF THE IMMUNE SYSTEM

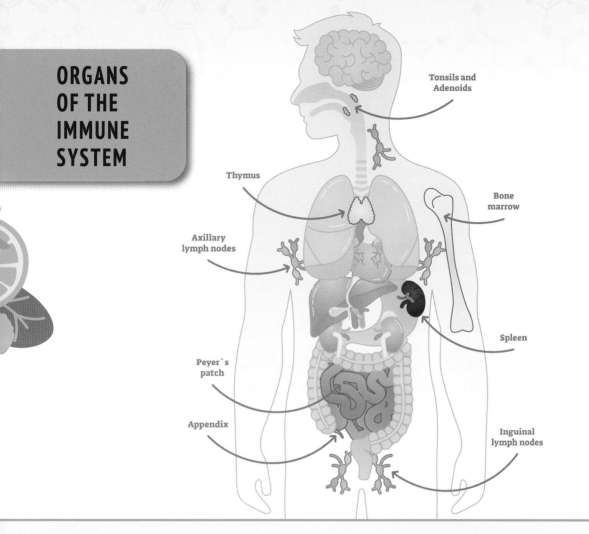

Tonsils and Adenoids

Thymus

Bone marrow

Axillary lymph nodes

Spleen

Peyer`s patch

Appendix

Inguinal lymph nodes

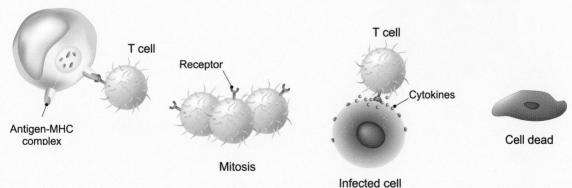

Antigen-MHC complex

T cell

Receptor

Mitosis

T cell

Cytokines

Infected cell

Cell dead

.

B cell

↓

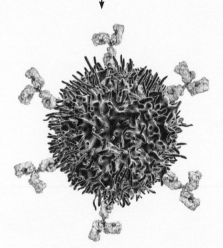

Memory B cell

ANTIBODY MEMORY BANK

Always Remember

The most important and powerful function of the acquired immune system is that the cells can "remember" invaders from past attacks. This is what allows the body to be able to fight off severe illness and infection. The quicker an immune system can respond and create an army of antibodies, the quicker it can disarm attackers and prevent damage.

Some B cells remain after an attack and become "memory B cells." They are able to produce antibodies for a long time. Memory cells are **dormant** after the first attack and circulate through the bloodstream. They are always on the lookout for the same enemy attacker. Unlike the first time a new invader is encountered, the second time the response from the immune system is not only faster, but also stronger. This means that with a second exposure, the symptoms of the illness from the virus or bacteria are usually much milder or are not noticeable at all.

Sometimes the immune memory lasts a lifetime. One exposure or one vaccination is enough to protect the body. This is true for pathogens that do not create different versions of themselves, called variants, very often. The virus that causes measles has basically stayed the same throughout history. One exposure is usually enough for a person to fight it off their entire life. Other antibodies only create an immune memory for a number of years. **Tetanus**, or lockjaw, is an infection caused by bacteria. Tetanus vaccination protection declines over time and boosters are needed. Other diseases such as influenza change and **mutate** very quickly. Even though the body may have antibodies for one type, another type may start spreading. That is why people are urged to get flu shots every year.

20

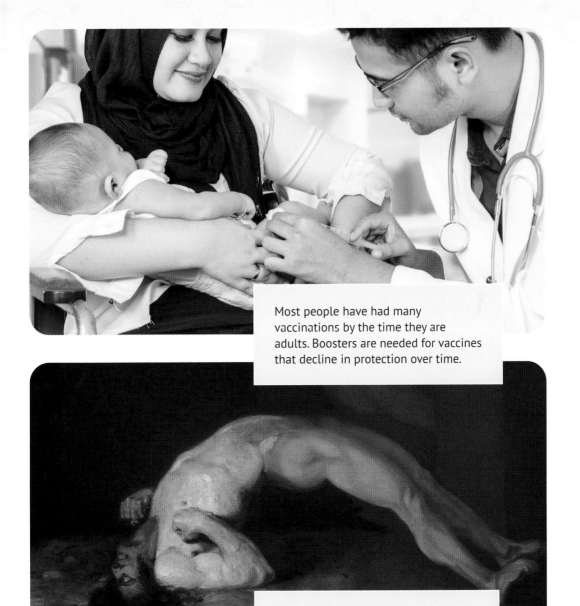

Most people have had many vaccinations by the time they are adults. Boosters are needed for vaccines that decline in protection over time.

Created by Scottish doctor and scientist Sir Charles Bell in 1809, this painting shows a man suffering muscle spasms from tetanus. The infection usually killed people. The tetanus vaccine wasn't developed until 1924.

The Lymphatic System

The lymphatic system is a network of vessels and nodes. The vessels are like a highway system around the body. The nodes are often collection points for white blood cells to act as lookouts for invaders.

The lymphatic vessels contain a clear fluid called lymph. Lymph is a collection of drainage fluids from organs and tissue that may contain **toxins**, waste, and other unwanted materials. The lymph passes through the lymph nodes where there are many white blood cells that can trap viruses, bacteria, and other invaders, including cancer cells, as they pass by. Cancer is a disease where cells grow uncontrollably. This is why doctors often check a person's lymph nodes to look for signs of cancer. There are hundreds of lymph nodes in the human body. They are located all over the body, including in the neck, chest, and under the arms.

Some of the organs connected with the lymphatic system, such as the spleen and thymus, don't just store these cells, they also develop them. Tonsils are large clumps of lymphatic cells found at the back of the throat. They are often the first line of defense for pathogens that enter the body through the nose or mouth. They can filter for dangerous invaders and, using the white blood cells stored in them, kill off invaders and flush them out using lymph.

Fact Check

Do swollen glands in your throat mean you're sick?

FACT: The swollen glands that people often refer to are usually enlarged lymph nodes. If these nodes are larger than usual or sore, it is a good indication that they are hard at work fighting infection.

Tonsils

Thymus

Mammary Plexus

Axillary Lymph Node

Thoracic Duct

Spleen

Intestinal Lymph Node

Large Intestine

Small Intestine

Appendix

Lymphatic Vessel

Inguinal Lymph Node

Bone Marrow

Lymphatic Vessel

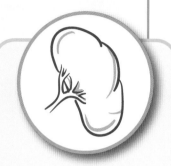

What Does the Spleen Do?

The spleen contains white blood cells and acts as a filter. It clears out old and damaged cells and pathogens in our bloodstream.

A Little Jab

Vaccinations have been around for more than 200 years. In 1796, the first smallpox vaccine was developed. Over the next 180 years, countries around the world worked to vaccinate all residents. In 1979, smallpox was officially declared **eradicated**. Not all vaccines have been able to wipe out a disease completely, but they have saved the lives of millions of people.

Vaccines work by giving the immune system a "heads-up" on the identity of a pathogen. There are three main types of vaccines. The first type contains pathogens that are dead. These are called inactivated vaccines. They do not produce as strong a reaction as live vaccines. Sometimes it takes booster shots to get the immune system to have lasting memory. Polio, rabies, and the flu vaccines are inactivated.

Live vaccines produce a much stronger reaction. Even though the pathogen is live, the virus or bacteria has been weakened so it cannot replicate or cause damage. This is called attenuated. Live attenuated vaccines create a strong and long-lasting immune response. Just one or two doses can offer lifelong protection. Measles, smallpox, and chicken pox are live attenuated vaccines.

Messenger RNA (mRNA) vaccines contain just the proteins that pathogens usually carry on their surface. This is enough for B cells to identify the pathogen and create antibodies. Because these vaccines do not carry the live virus, there is no risk of getting the disease. Several COVID-19 vaccines use this process.

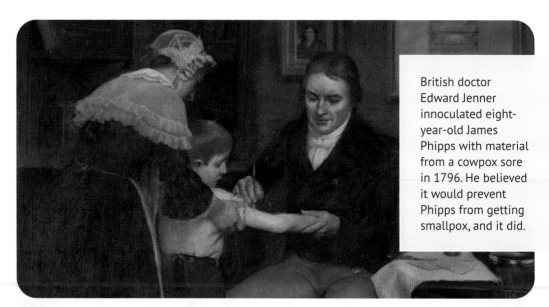

British doctor Edward Jenner innoculated eight-year-old James Phipps with material from a cowpox sore in 1796. He believed it would prevent Phipps from getting smallpox, and it did.

In North America, most babies start receiving vaccinations at around two months old. These protect them from a number of diseases that used to kill or permanently harm children, including polio.

Fact Check

Can you get the flu from a flu vaccine?

FACT: Sometimes people can feel symptoms such as a slight fever, aches, or a headache after a vaccine. These are not signs of illness, but instead are signs of the immune system at work, trying to fight off what it thinks is a dangerous pathogen.

CHAPTER 3

When It Doesn't Work

Like any network with lots of different parts, sometimes the immune system breaks down. Immune system disorders can be the result of:

- Being born with a weak immune system. This is called primary immunodeficiency.

- Having an immune system that is too active. This may show as allergic reactions.

- Getting a disease that weakens your immune system. This is called acquired immunodeficiency.

- Having an immune system that turns against you. This is called autoimmune disease.

People who have primary immunodeficiency have less ability to fight infections.

People born with primary immunodeficiency (PI) have an immune system that does not work properly. PI causes infections such as ear infections, sinus infections, pneumonia, bronchitis, skin infections, and many others that happen more often. These infections tend to last longer than they do for most people and they do not respond easily to **antibiotic** medications. People with PI may need to be hospitalized to treat the infections.

There are more than 400 different types of PI. Some are more severe than others. Those with mild problems may not notice anything wrong until they are adults. Others have a more severe type that can cause problems from birth. Children born with PI are in constant danger from bacteria, viruses, and fungi.

Severe combined immunodeficiency (SCID) is the most severe type of PI. Children suffering from SCID do not form properly working B and T cells. This disorder is sometimes called "bubble baby disease" because these children had to be kept in plastic, **sterile** environments. Today most children with SCID receive a stem cell transplant so their bone marrow can begin to make both kinds of white blood cells on its own.

David Vetter was born with SCID in 1971. He lived in a sterile environment to lessen the chance of viruses harming him. He died at 12 after an unsuccessful bone marrow transplant. Medicine has advanced over time. Now children with SCID get early transplants.

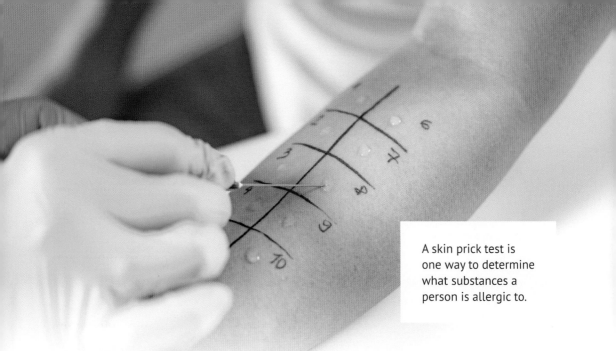

A skin prick test is one way to determine what substances a person is allergic to.

Allergies and Reactions

An immune system that responds strongly to harmless substances in the environment is called an overactive immune system. People who suffer from allergies have this type of problem. These normally harmless substances are called allergens. Common allergens are dust, mold, or some foods.

Allergic disease is one of the most common **chronic** health conditions in the world. About 40 percent of people in the world suffer from some sort of allergy. Symptoms can range from mild to life-threatening. Mild symptoms include wheezing, itchy or watery eyes, and a runny nose. Allergies to dust or pet **dander** often cause these mild but annoying reactions. Sometimes mild allergic reactions only happen at certain times of the year, such as with plant allergies. Pollen allergies happen in the spring when plants release it, and ragweed allergies tend to occur in the fall when the plants are mature.

Some allergies cause breathing problems such as asthma. Asthma occurs when your airways swell so less air can move in and out. Dust mites and pollen are common allergens that can cause asthma. Allergic disease can also cause a skin condition called eczema. Eczema makes your skin red and itchy. Common triggers are soaps or detergents, and grasses or pollen.

Anaphylaxis is the name given to a severe, life-threatening allergic reaction. This reaction causes the immune system to release a flood of chemicals very quickly. People have trouble breathing and need medical treatment immediately. Certain food allergies or insect stings can result in anaphylaxis.

Can you outgrow an allergy?

FACT: Yes, it is possible to outgrow allergies. Sometimes this happens naturally. Usually repeated small doses of an allergen can teach the immune system to **tolerate** it. Outgrowing an allergy happens most often with mild allergic reactions.

Immune Deficiencies

Acquired immune deficiency can be the result of disease or treatment for disease. These effects can be temporary or permanent. Sometimes a weakened immune system is necessary to help the health of a patient.

People suffering from cancer often have to undergo chemotherapy treatment. The chemicals used to kill cancer cells can lower the number of white blood cells that help fight infection. This is often a temporary effect that will reverse once the treatment ends. Sometimes medications are used to **suppress** the immune system on purpose. People who have an **organ transplant** are in danger of their immune system identifying the transplant as foreign tissue. This will cause the immune system to target and attack the healthy organ. Transplant patients are given medications that suppress their immune system. They have to take this medication for the rest of their life.

Diseases can also cause acquired immune deficiency. The measles, flu, or mononucleosis (commonly called mono) can cause permanent damage to the immune system. Studies show that the measles virus can wipe out the immune system memory for years after it arrives. This leaves the body at risk to infections that would normally be killed off easily.

The Human Immunodeficiency Virus (HIV) is one of the most dangerous viruses for the immune system. The virus is passed in body fluids from one person to another. HIV destroys T cells. Without T cells, the body cannot easily and quickly fight off other diseases. It leaves the person at risk for all kinds of infections and cancer. Once the virus has damaged the immune system, the person develops Acquired Immune Deficiency Syndrome, or AIDS. There is no cure or vaccine for the virus yet. Drugs can help prevent the virus from replicating and damaging the immune system further.

Chemotherapy kills cancer cells as well as other cells. During treatment, and for a time after, cancer patients have little to no immunity to diseases.

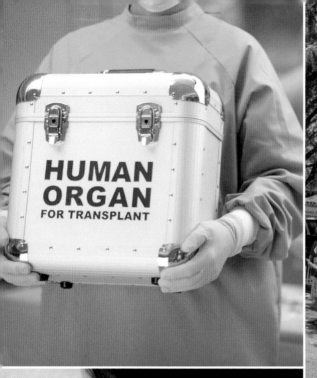

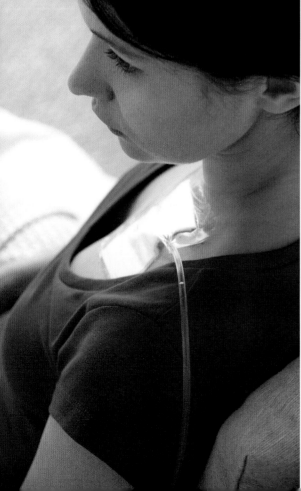

HIV weakens the immune system. If left untreated, it can lead to AIDS, a disease that has killed millions of people in the decades since it was identified.

Autoimmune Diseases

Autoimmune disease happens when the immune system wrongfully identifies its own body's cells as invaders and attacks them. Some of the symptoms that this creates can be serious. Scientists have not fully unlocked the reasons why autoimmune diseases happen. One theory is that certain pathogens may trigger changes that confuse the immune system.

Rheumatoid arthritis is an autoimmune disease. The immune system attacks healthy cells mostly in the joints. The tissue swells and causes severe pain. Over time, this inflammation can result in permanent damage and can even cause the joint to become misshapen. Lupus is another autoimmune disease that causes pain and **inflammation**. It can affect the brain, heart, joints, skin, kidneys, blood cells, and lungs. Multiple sclerosis (MS) is a chronic disease where the immune system attacks the body's nerve fibers in the brain and **spinal cord**. This can change the signals sent to and from the brain.

Diabetes is a disease that affects the body's ability to process sugar. Insulin is a **hormone** produced by the pancreas that helps control the sugar in the body. With diabetes, either the body doesn't produce any or enough insulin, or it can't properly use the insulin it does produce. Too much blood sugar can damage organs, blood vessels, and nerves. The most severe type of diabetes is type 1. It is an autoimmune disease where the immune system attacks the pancreas. About 463 million people around the world suffer from some form of diabetes.

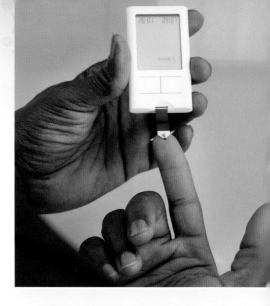

Autoimmune diseases are treated with medications and often lifestyle changes so that people can live longer and healthier lives.

Celiac Disease

Gluten is the name for proteins found in different grains, such as wheat and rye. Celiac disease results in people not being able to process gluten in their intestines because their immune system has caused damage. The only treatment for those who have it is to avoid eating any gluten in their diet.

GLUTEN FREE

CHAPTER 4

Keeping the System Healthy

Keeping your immune system healthy is not as straightforward as we'd like it to be. That is because it is a whole system—a network of different organs, tissue, and cells. There are so many different parts, in so many places in the body, that one treatment or action cannot affect all of it.

Exercise helps the body and mind cope with stress. Stress plays havoc with the immune system.

The best way to protect the immune system is to have a healthy lifestyle overall. This includes getting plenty of sleep. When you sleep, your body does a lot of repairing and healing. Getting enough exercise is also important. Regular exercise lowers the level of the hormone cortisol. Too much cortisol in the body can **restrict** the immune system.

Drinking water is an important part of keeping healthy. Water is essential for all body functions as it carries nutrients and oxygen to cells. This will keep the organs that produce immune cells efficient and functioning. Fluids transport white blood cells around the body and drinking enough water keeps the level of these fluids high.

Although the job of the immune system is to fight off infection and disease, avoiding **preventable** infections and diseases is key. This is because certain diseases can weaken the system and make it vulnerable to another infection, fungus, or virus. Prevention can be done by remembering to wash your hands, keeping up to date with vaccinations, and following food safety rules when cooking and eating.

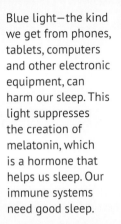

Blue light—the kind we get from phones, tablets, computers and other electronic equipment, can harm our sleep. This light suppresses the creation of melatonin, which is a hormone that helps us sleep. Our immune systems need good sleep.

Fact Check

Does being cold weaken your immune system and cause you to catch a cold or flu?

FACT: Researchers have studied this. So far there is no research to back this up. Being chilled or cold for a short period does not seem to lead to more colds or flu infections. Instead, cold weather means more people stay indoors, where viruses spread more easily.

Diet and Nutrients

The saying "you are what you eat" refers to the fact that the nutrients in your food are what fuels your body. Every cell, tissue, and organ needs certain vitamins and minerals in order to work well.

The best way to make sure the immune system has all the different **micronutrients** it needs is to eat a wide variety of fruits, vegetables, and protein. Spinach is high in iron, which helps in the development of white blood cells. Oranges contain vitamin C, which helps phagocytes kill invaders. Protein found in meats and eggs helps in the sending and receiving of messages between the cells that activate the immune system.

Some foods, such as blueberries, cherries, and kale contain large amounts of compounds called antioxidants. Antioxidants bind to harmful molecules called "free radicals." Free radicals can destroy other cells, tissue, and organs. Eating foods high in antioxidants stabilizes and prevents damage in the body.

Researchers have noted that people living in poverty who lack a good diet are more vulnerable to infection. Studies show that children who grow up **malnourished** are more likely to develop autoimmune disorders as adults, such as rheumatoid arthritis.

People in North America and Asia lead the world in taking vitamin and mineral supplements.

Health in a Pill?

Dietary supplements are pills or liquids that contain trace minerals, vitamins, or herbs. Sometimes food grown in certain areas or in poor soil does not have as much of the vitamins and minerals as usual. So eating this food still might not provide our bodies with what they need. Supplements are one way people can get these micronutrients that they cannot get in their diet.

A healthy diet includes plenty of vegetables, fruits, and protein. Experts say they can be canned, frozen, dried, or fresh.

Fact Check

Do soap and water "kill" viruses?

FACT: They don't, but what they do is cover the virus with the fats in soap so they can't cling on. Experts say hands should be lathered up for 30 seconds and then rinsed to wash the virus down the drain.

CHAPTER 5

Looking to the Future

The immune system is far from being completely understood. Researchers are still studying both the innate and acquired systems.

Genes and Immunity

Scientists are looking into whether or not we pass on some immunity through our genes. Genes are made of chemical building blocks and they carry the information that tells our body how to grow, act, and change. Genes are found in every cell in our body. If the chemicals are not in the correct order, the gene could act very differently than it is supposed to. Being able to fix or replace genes is called gene therapy.

Scientists are studying whether immunity to specific diseases might also be passed on through genes. Studies show that there is a certain gene in about 7 percent of people from **Sub-Saharan Africa** that gives them protection from some strains of malaria. Malaria is a serious disease that infects red blood cells. It causes 1 to 3 million deaths each year. Replicating this gene and using it to help people at risk could reduce death and disease from malaria around the world.

Gene therapy may provide a cure for other immune problems. For children suffering from SCID, gene therapy is being explored as a way to allow their bone marrow to begin making white blood cells. Some people have a gene that is known to cause a lack of antibodies. Now that scientists have identified it, they can work on gene therapy to fix it.

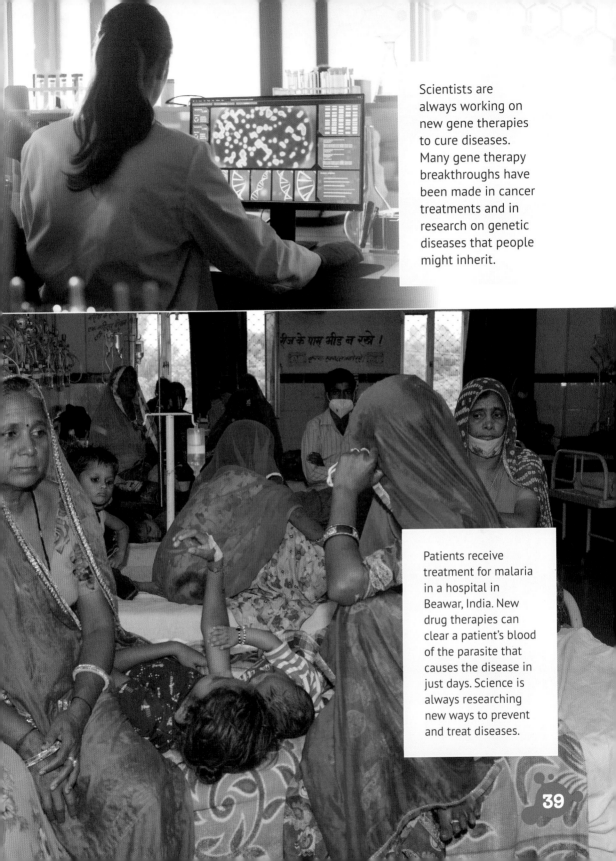

Scientists are always working on new gene therapies to cure diseases. Many gene therapy breakthroughs have been made in cancer treatments and in research on genetic diseases that people might inherit.

Patients receive treatment for malaria in a hospital in Beawar, India. New drug therapies can clear a patient's blood of the parasite that causes the disease in just days. Science is always researching new ways to prevent and treat diseases.

The Way Forward

Research is unlocking more mysteries of the immune system, allowing for new treatments for diseases and new vaccines. People suffering from diabetes and cancer may have hope for a longer, healthier life.

With diabetes, the body's own T cells attack the insulin-producing cells in the pancreas. Without insulin to process sugar, it collects in the body's bloodstream. Too much sugar affects **arteries** all over the body. It causes the walls of the arteries to thicken and grow stiff. This can lead to high blood pressure, heart attacks, and strokes.

Researchers noticed that healthy people have some special "peacekeeping" T cells called Tregs. These cells stop false alarms in the immune system where it attacks its own cells. People suffering from type 1 diabetes do not have enough of this type of T cell. Scientists are testing medications that promote the development of more Tregs in diabetics.

Multiple sclerosis (MS) is a central nervous system disease that occurs when the immune system attacks the brain and spinal cord. New forms of gene therapy have the potential to stop the disease's immune response. It can take years for a new therapy to be tested and made available to people with a disease.

A group physical therapy session for people with multiple sclerosis.

Fact Check

You cannot prevent diabetes

FACT: While type 1 diabetes has its roots in a faulty immune system, type 2 diabetes is preventable. Being overweight, unhealthy eating habits, and lack of exercise all contribute. By watching your diet, exercise, and weight, type 2 diabetes can be prevented, or at least delayed.

Leading an active life is important for both the prevention and treatment of type 2 diabetes. This includes exercise, diet, and monitoring the disease to keep it under control.

Cancer research is ongoing. Each year, researchers know more and develop new and better treatments. Many new treatments are targeted at individuals and their specific type of cancer.

Research Continues

Cancer is one of the leading causes of death in North America. Discovering new ways to help the immune system fight cancer is extremely important. Leukemia is a cancer of the blood and bone marrow. Scientists have discovered that leukemia cells carry a protein that helps the cancer cells multiply. They are working on treatments to deactivate this protein to prevent leukemia cells from spreading.

Other research is working on developing **personalized** vaccines for cancer. The mutations that cancer causes in cells is different in each person. Scientists are working on developing vaccines that are specific to the cancer cells in individuals.

Key Figures

Researchers James Allison and Tasuku Honjo won the 2018 Nobel Prize in Physiology or Medicine for work on cancer immunotherapy. They noticed that cancer cells found a way to **hijack** proteins that suppress the immune system after an infection, allowing the cancer cells to spread. Allison and Honjo found a way to get the immune system to ignore those proteins and continue to attack and kill cancer cells.

New Vaccines

Vaccines are one of the most successful ways to prevent diseases. The World Health Organization (WHO) estimates that vaccines prevent 2 to 3 million deaths each year. New discoveries are making vaccines even safer and more effective.

New research has found a nanoparticle that plays a part in immune response. Nanoparticles are so small they can only be seen with the most powerful microscopes. This tiny particle has been shown to create a stronger reaction when the signal goes out to create B and T cells. In vaccines, this would lead to a stronger and longer-lasting cell memory.

In order to produce millions of vaccines, the proteins the immune system recognizes and mounts a defense against have to be replicated in laboratories. This is mostly done in animal cells. This has limitations. The cells are expensive to get. Sometimes the animals carry other bacteria or viruses. Replicating and testing takes a long time. Even more importantly, some people have allergies to certain animal products that are used for vaccine production, such as chicken eggs.

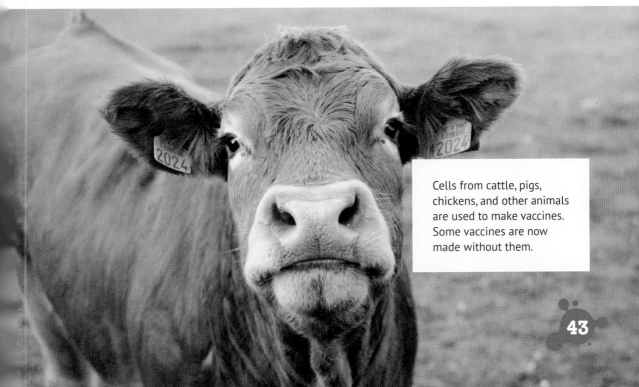

Cells from cattle, pigs, chickens, and other animals are used to make vaccines. Some vaccines are now made without them.

43

Plant Cell Vaccines

A company called Medicago in Quebec, Canada, is working on changing this. Instead of animal cells, they are growing proteins in plant cells. Using plants produces vaccines faster and reduces some of the problems associated with using animal cells. Plants such as Nicotiana benthamiana, commonly known as benth, can produce enough of the specific protein in five to six weeks instead of four to six months for animal cell-based production. Protein cells developed from animals must be kept frozen at specific temperatures. Plant-based ones can be kept in a refrigerator. This makes them easier to transport and store. Medicago has developed a COVID-19 vaccine called COVIFENZ for use in the future. It has also worked on vaccines for other viruses, including seasonal flu. Research is ongoing for cancer vaccines.

Plant cells are being used in biotechnology research to develop new drugs for diseases that affect the immune system.

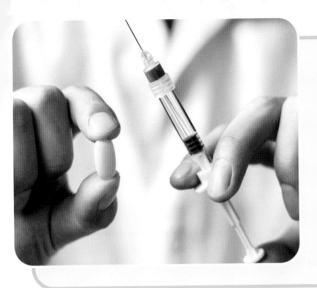

New Fixes for Needle Anxiety

Scientists are working on new vaccines in pill and liquid form for those who struggle with needle anxiety. The pill and liquid vaccines work by engaging the immune system in the gut.

COVIFENZ was developed during the COVID-19 pandemic and approved for use in Canada in February 2022.

Glossary

acquired Obtained or developed

activated Started working

antibiotic A medicine that destroys microorganisms

antibodies Y-shaped proteins that attach to pathogens

arteries Tubes that carry blood through the body

bacteria A group of very small living things that often causes disease

beneficial Helpful, not harmful

chronic Happening again and again over a long period of time

dander Small bits of hair, fur, or skin shed by animals

dormant Not active

eliminate To get rid of

encountered Met

engulfing Surrounding and covering

eradicated Did away with completely

germs Microorganisms that cause disease

gland A group of cells that produces chemicals for use in the body

hijack To take over without permission

hormone A chemical substance made in the body

inflammation A condition where part of the body is swollen, hot, and painful

inherited Passed from parent to child through genes

innate Born with

inoculation To implant a disease on purpose to activate the immune system

malnourished Not getting a proper amount of food, vitamins, and minerals

micronutrients Tiny amounts of elements needed for good growth and development

mutate To change into another form

nodes Small bean-shaped groups of cells that work together

organ transplant Receiving a new body part to replace a damaged one

organisms Living things

pandemic A disease that affects the whole world at the same time

personalized Designed to someone's individual needs

plague A contagious bacterial disease

preventable Able to be avoided

replicate To make exact copies

restrict To put a limit on

saliva The watery liquid your mouth produces

shaman A religious person who performs rituals

species A group of animals or plants that are similar and can produce young

spinal cord The bundle of nerves found inside the backbone

sterile Containing no pathogens

Sub-Saharan Africa Countries in Africa that lie south of the Sahara Desert

suppress To keep from working or developing

tetanus A disease that can cause the jaw to seize and make it hard to eat or breathe

theory Carefully thought out ideas that explain things that are observed in science

tolerate To put up with

toxins Poison or venom from a plant or animal

Learning More

BOOKS

Bennett, Howard. *The Fantastic Body: What Makes You Tick & How You Get Sick*. Rodale Kids, 2017.

Koch, Falynn. *Science Comics: Plagues: The Microscopic Battlefield*. First Second, 2017.

Mould, Steve. *The Bacteria Book: The Big World of Really Tiny Microbes*. DK Children, 2018.

WEBSITES

A to Z Kids Stuff talks all about germs in this fun video:
https://www.atozkidsstuff.com/health.html

Learn all about viruses and bacteria with this PBS video:
https://www.pbs.org/video/viruses-virus-or-bacteria-pds2io/

Take a quiz with History of Vaccines to see how much you know about how vaccines work:
https://www.historyofvaccines.org/content/how-vaccines-work

Index

About the Author

Natalie Hyde has written more than 100 fiction and nonfiction books for kids. She has always been fascinated by the extraordinary machine we call the human body. Natalie lives with her family, their dog Louie, and a flock of Rhode Island Red chickens called "The Ladies."